D0459393

Let's Play Tag!

- Read the Page
- Read the Story
- Game
- Sound It / Say It
- Repeat
- Stop

Get-Ready Words

anemone	ocean
anglerfish	school
current	sharks
jellyfish	teacher
moonfish	tentacles

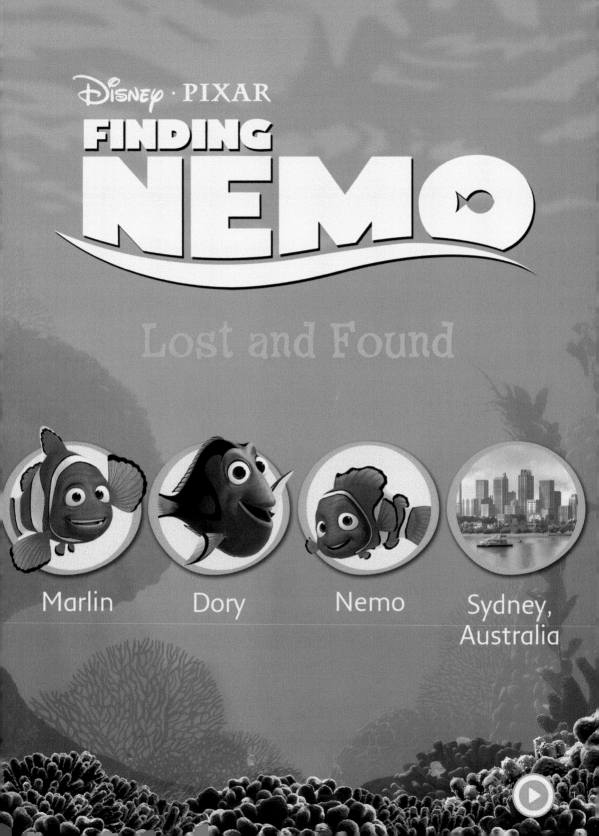

 Nemo lives in a sea anemone.
He lives with his dad, Marlin.

Nemo wants to go to school.
His dad wants him to wait.

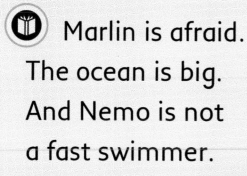 Marlin is afraid.
The ocean is big.
And Nemo is not
a fast swimmer.

What if Nemo gets hurt?

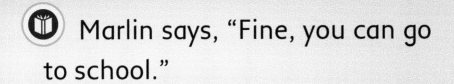 Marlin says, "Fine, you can go to school."

Nemo meets his teacher.

"Dad, you can go now," Nemo says.

Marlin sees the class go to the Drop-off!

Marlin swims after Nemo.

Nemo wants to be brave.
He swims to a boat. A scuba
diver grabs Nemo.

Marlin tries to save
him. He is stopped
by a different
scuba diver.

Nemo is gone.
He is on the boat.

Marlin swims fast.
He cannot catch up.

Where did the boat go?

A fish named Dory
had seen the boat.

Marlin and Dory go
to find Nemo.

Marlin and Dory swim deeper into the blue ocean. Marlin is afraid.

Where is Nemo?

"Just keep swimming," Dory says.

Dory and Marlin
meet a lot of creatures.
Sharks chase them!

Anglerfish chase
them too!

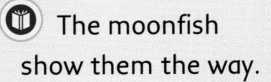

The moonfish
show them the way.

They must go to
Sydney, Australia!

Dory and Marlin swim into a jellyfish forest. Jellyfish can sting.

"Do not touch the
tentacles," Marlin tells Dory.

A turtle helps
Dory and Marlin.

They swim on
the current to
Sydney, Australia.

"Dad!" says Nemo.

Nemo and Marlin hug.

They go back home.

Dory goes with
them. Marlin and
Nemo are happy.

Words You're Learning

Short Vowels

Short a Words	Short e Words	Short i Words	Short o Words	Short u Words
and	get	big	not	just
can	help	fish	on	up
dad	tell	him	stop	
grab		his		
		swim		
		with		

Long Vowels

Long a Words	Long e Words	Long i Words	Long o Words	Long u Words
brave	deep	fine	boat	blue
save	he		go	
wait	keep		home	
	meet			
	see			

Sight Words

are	of	to	what
different	say	too	where
do	the	touch	you
gone	they	wants	
lives